Healing Aft

Loss

Of A

Father

For

Daughters

How To Deal With Grief Over The Death, Abandonment, Or Emotional Absence Of A Father, Heal From The Pain, And Find New Strength And Calm Within You

Jennifer Worral

Copyright © 2023. Jennifer Worral.

All Rights Reserved.

INTRODUCTION — 4

CHAPTER ONE — 8

UNDERSTANDING THE DEEP AND COMPLEX EMOTIONAL BURDEN OF LOSING A FATHER FOR DAUGHTERS — 8
EXAMINING THE MANY FACETS OF FATHER LOSS FOR DAUGHTERS — 11
THE EIGHT COMMON EMOTIONS DAUGHTERS FEEL AFTER THE LOSS OF A FATHER — 15

CHAPTER TWO — 22

UNDERSTANDING THE SPECIAL ROLES FATHERS PLAY IN THE LIVES OF THEIR DAUGHTERS — 22

CHAPTER THREE — 32

HOW SOCIAL, CULTURAL, AND FAMILY FACTORS AFFECT HOW DAUGHTER GRIEF THE LOSS OF A FATHER — 32

CHAPTER FOUR — 40

UNDERSTANDING THE DIFFERENT STAGES OF GRIEF FOR DAUGHTERS AFTER THE LOSS OF A FATHER — 40

CHAPTER FIVE — 54

UNDERSTANDING THE DIFFERENT CHALLENGES DAUGHTERS FACE AFTER THE LOSS OF A FATHER — 54

CHAPTER SIX — 64

HOW THE LOSS OF A FATHER IMPACTS ON DAUGHTERS IN THEIR INTIMATE RELATIONSHIP, FRIENDSHIPS, AND FAMILY RELATIONSHIPS — 64

CHAPTER SEVEN — 70

DIFFERENT ROLES AND RESPONSIBILITIES TAKEN ON BY ADULT DAUGHTERS AFTER THE LOSS OF A FATHER — 70

CHAPTER EIGHT — 78

6 EFFECTIVE STRATEGIES ON COPING WITH THE LOSS OF A FATHER FOR DAUGHTERS — 78

CHAPTER NINE — 100

13 PROFOUND WAYS DAUGHTERS CAN HONOR AND PRESERVE THE MEMORIES OF THEIR FATHERS — 100

CONCLUSION — 108

INTRODUCTION

The loss of a father is an intensely traumatic experience that can profoundly alter the emotional landscape of adult daughters. It is a journey through the wilderness of grief, where the landscape is covered with complex emotions, treasured memories, and a yearning for the lost presence of a father.

In the aftermath of a father's loss, the emotional landscape can be chaotic and unpredictable. It is a terrain where grief coexists with love, sadness, anger, and a wide range of other difficult emotions. This book explores the complex levels of the grieving process and acknowledges the devastating impacts of losing a father on daughters. It inspires adult daughters to set out on a journey of self-discovery, reflection, and healing, as they negotiate the difficult landscape of grief.

The chapters in this book explore the many facets of father loss, including the special bond that exists between fathers and daughters, the importance of this relationship in shaping identity and emotional well-being, and the role that fathers play in providing emotional support and guidance to their daughters. By looking at various types of father loss, such as death, absence, or estrangement, and identifying the many situations and experiences that contribute to father loss, daughters will gain a deeper understanding of their own experiences and find consolation in knowing they are not alone.

The book digs deeper into the grieving process, exploring the emotional stages of shock, denial, anger, bargaining, depression, and acceptance. In order to help adult daughters navigate the complexity of their grieving process, each stage is sensitively and insightfully examined, while strategies and compassionate guidance are provided.

As the book progresses, it addresses the specific challenges faced by adult daughters grieving the loss of a father, covering the impact on their sense of identity, self-worth, and ability to develop a strong sense of self in the absence of a father's presence. It examines the long-term effects of father loss on self-esteem and personal growth while offering strategies to foster healing, resilience, and the discovery of a renewed sense of meaning and purpose.

The book acknowledges that the process of grieving is not linear and that the emotional journey varies in duration and intensity. It explores how cultural, societal, and familial factors influence emotional responses to grief and highlights the importance of self-care, seeking emotional support, and engaging in meaningful activities as integral parts of the healing process. It also offers guidance on how to navigate personal and familial relationships in the aftermath of a father's loss, acknowledging the challenges that arise and revealing strategies for maintaining positive connections.

Throughout the book, profound insights and practical solutions merge to provide a complete and comprehensive approach to healing. This book primarily aims to offer relief, understanding, and hope to adult daughters who are grieving the loss of their fathers. It is a guide through the wilderness of grief, shedding light on the path towards healing, self-discovery, and a renewed sense of purpose. Together, let us travel this emotional terrain, honor our fathers' memories, and find strength and resilience in the face of loss.

CHAPTER ONE

Understanding the Deep and Complex Emotional Burden of Losing a Father For Daughters

The experience of losing a father can have a deep and long-lasting effect on a person's emotional health. It is a loss that can affect every facet of one's life and leaves a deep mark on the heart and soul. Understanding the grieving process and starting down the path to healing require knowledge of the depth and complexity of the emotional impact the loss of a father can cause a daughter.

First and foremost, losing a father brings on a wide range of strong emotions. The memories of shared experiences, conversations, and once-shared love can become entwined with grief, sadness, and longing, which become constant companions for the daughter. The emotional impact can show up in a variety of ways, including intense sadness and emptiness as well as emotions of guilt, rage, and confusion. It's crucial to understand that there is no right or wrong way to grieve and that everyone's emotional landscape is different.

The emotional effects of losing a father go beyond the period of grieving. It has the power to significantly change a daughter's identity and sense of self. Fathers often act as a source of support, guidance, and a mirror through which we view ourselves. In his absence, a daughter might begin to wonder about her identity, purpose, and position in the universe. The loss may upend the basis on which her self-esteem and confidence are built, resulting in a period of introspection and the reinvention of her goals.

The complex dynamics of the father-daughter relationship can add to the emotional impact. Fathers perform multiple roles in their daughters' lives, including protectors, role models, and providers of unconditional love. They support the emotional growth, sense of value, and worldview of their daughters. Losing a father involves losing not only his physical presence but also the continual reassurance and support that he provided. This profound absence can leave an emptiness that is difficult to fill.

Healing begins with acknowledging the significant and complicated emotional effects of losing a father. It enables daughters to realize the intensity of their emotions, validate their experiences, and seek help from others who have been through similar situations. By recognizing the emotional impact, daughters can start to make sense of their emotions, find comfort in other people's stories and experiences, and allow themselves to grow and be able to carry on their father's legacy in their own special way.

Examining The Many Facets Of Father Loss For Daughters

Father loss is a very personal experience that can result from a wide variety of different situations. We may better respect the complexity of a daughter's journey and the unique difficulties she encounters when we understand and acknowledge the varied situations and experiences that can lead to father loss. By understanding the diverse nature of father loss, we can encourage empathy, support, and a more inclusive approach to healing and recovery.

That said, here are many situations that can lead to the loss of a father for daughters:

1. Death:

The most well-known type of father loss is death. This may be the result of unforeseen events, illnesses, natural causes, or accidents. Every daughter's experience of losing a father to death is unique, shaped by the circumstances surrounding the loss, the relationship shared, and the grieving process of the daughter. Recognizing the variety of experiences daughters have with the death of a father helps to establish a safe space where they can share their stories, pay tribute to their fathers' memories, and look for comfort and help within a supportive community.

2. Divorce Or Separation:

A daughter who experiences a divorce or separation may no longer have her father in her life. The breakdown of the parental relationship can lead to significant changes in family dynamics which often leaves the daughter without a reliable father figure. Daughters could struggle with the loss of daily interaction, shared memories, and the emotional support their fathers provided. Recognizing the impact of divorce or separation as a contributing factor to father loss acknowledges the experiences of daughters facing these circumstances and points out the need for support and healing in such circumstances.

3. Deployment Or Work-Related Absence:

Fathers who are deployed or who have busy work schedules may spend a significant amount of time away from their daughters. Both fathers and daughters may experience feelings of loss, longing, and emotional strain as a result of the separation brought on by deployment or work-related absences. Understanding the difficulties daughters encounter in these situations and the sacrifices made by fathers helps to foster empathy and emphasizes the need to sustain interactions despite physical distance.

4. Emotional Disconnection Or Absence:

The absence of a true emotional connection between fathers and daughters can also result in father loss. This might be the result of things like emotional unavailability, toxic relationships, or a lack of bonding. Emotional disconnection can lead to feelings of loss, unfulfilled needs, and a longing for a deeper connection for daughters. Acknowledging emotional disconnection or absence as a form of father loss validates the experiences of daughters who may be dealing with feelings of abandonment, rejection, or unsatisfied emotional needs.

5. Estrangement:

Estrangement is a breakdown in the father-daughter relationship, which often leads to a long period of disconnection. It could result from unsolved conflicts, opposing values, or other difficult situations. Estrangement can result in significant emotional suffering, loss, and feelings of rejection. Understanding estrangement as a form of father loss takes into account the intricacy of family relationships and the effects broken bonds can have on daughters' lives. It also highlights the importance of finding ways to reconcile when it's possible and desired, as well as the necessity for support and healing.

The Eight Common Emotions Daughters Feel After The Loss Of A Father

The loss of a father can trigger a wide range of emotional responses in adult daughters. These feelings are a natural reaction to the intense sense of loss and the crucial role that fathers often play in their lives. Examining these natural emotional responses will help us understand the difficult grieving process that adult daughters go through.

The emotions that can be triggered by the loss of a father include:

1. Grief:

Grief is a basic and pervasive emotion felt when a father is lost. It includes a profound feeling of sorrow, longing, and emptiness. Adult daughters could be saddened by their father's absence and lament the loss of his physical support, guidance, and influence. Grief can present itself in a variety of ways, including weeping, wishing for their father, or experiencing waves of profound anguish. It's critical for adult daughters to give themselves the permission to grieve and to look for help as they deal with this intense emotion.

2. Sadness:

Another common emotional response to losing a father is sadness. It's possible for adult daughters to experience intense sadness over the loss of their fathers, as they go through the highs and lows of life without them. Reminders of their fathers, such as important events or treasured memories, can trigger the feeling of sadness in daughters. It is crucial that daughters allow themselves the space to feel and express their sadness as they come to terms with their loss.

3. Anger:

Anger is a complex emotion that might emerge after the loss of a father. Daughters may harbor resentment toward their fathers for abandoning them, perceived shortcomings, or unresolved conflicts in their relationship. They might also harbor resentment toward events or people connected to the loss of their father. This anger may be quite intense and take many forms, including frustration, discontent, or even bitterness.

4. Guilt:

Daughters who lose their fathers may experience guilt for a variety of reasons, including regretting past actions or choices, feeling that they did not spend enough time with their fathers, or feeling responsible for their fathers' wellbeing. Being overwhelmed by guilt could lead to self-blame or a protracted feeling of remorse. It is crucial for daughters to understand that guilt is a natural part of grieving and to work toward self-forgiveness and self-compassion.

5. Regret:

Another common emotional response that adult daughters may go through after the loss of a father is regret. They may find themselves thinking back on missed opportunities, unsaid words, or things they did not do for their fathers. Regret can be more painful when there are unresolved conflicts or damaged relationships with their fathers. The knowledge that they are no longer able to address or atone for these regrets could make daughters feel sadder and more grieved.

6. Longing:

A deep emotional response felt by many adult daughters after the loss of a father is an intense need for their father's presence and company. They could long for the comfort, guidance, and unwavering support that their fathers provided them. This need is especially strong during key life events like as graduations, weddings, or the birth of children, when they are heavily aware of their fathers' absence.

7. Confusion And Disorientation:

A daughter's feeling of stability and comfort can be disrupted by the loss of her father. As daughters navigate a world without their fathers, they may feel lost or confused. The absence of a father's guidance and influence may lead daughters to question their own identities, values, and capacity for making decisions. It's crucial for daughters to give themselves time and space to adjust to this new reality while also looking for support and engaging in self-reflection to reclaim their sense of identity and determine their own path.

8. Mixed Emotions:

Adult daughters may go through a wide range of emotions all at once, with their emotions changing and shifting as time goes on. Within a short period of time, they can notice themselves swinging between sadness, anger, guilt, and longing. This emotional complexity can be frustrating and overwhelming, leaving daughters emotionally exhausted. It is crucial for daughters to understand and embrace the fleeting nature of their emotions, and allow themselves to feel and express them without fear of judgment.

By acknowledging and understanding these common emotional reactions to the loss of a father, adult daughters can better understand their own emotional landscape.

CHAPTER TWO

Understanding The Special Roles Fathers Play In The Lives Of Their Daughters

The relationship between fathers and their daughters is always unique and uncommon, and it occupies a special place in the hearts of both. It is a bond that is defined by love, empathy, and a special understanding. We can better understand the depth, importance, and deep influence of the special relationship that exists between fathers and their daughters by taking a closer look at the roles a father can play when raising a girl child:

1. Unconditional Love And Protection:

Fathers are often seen as the protectors of their daughters, providing them with a sense of safety and security. The relationship is founded on unconditional love, where daughters are treated with respect and treasured for who they are. In times of vulnerability and difficulty, fathers provide a place of safety by offering encouragement and assurance.

2. Serving As Role Models And Mentors:

Fathers have a significant impact on the lives of their daughters by acting as mentors and role models. They influence their daughters' beliefs, attitudes, and ambitions through imparting knowledge, values, and life lessons. As they traverse the difficulties of life, fathers serve as a shining example of honesty, courage, and persistence for their daughters.

3. Emotional Support And Nurturing:

Fathers play a crucial role in the emotional development of their daughters. They give a listening ear, empathy, and understanding, as well as a shoulder to lean on. The emotional connection that the father-daughter relationship creates allows daughters to freely share their thoughts, fears, and aspirations with their fathers. Fathers encourage their daughters' emotional development by helping them build mental resilience and a positive self-image.

4. Shared Interests And Quality Time:

Shared interests and special times spent together are important components of the special relationship between fathers and daughters. These shared experiences, whether they include hobbies, sports, or other activities, forge bonds and leave enduring memories. Spending quality time with fathers cultivates a sense of connection, which deepens their mutual love and understanding between them and their daughters.

5. Supportive And Empowering Relationships:

Fathers play an important role in their daughters' self-esteem and confidence. They provide their daughters with continuous support and inspiration, enabling them to achieve their goals. Fathers instill a sense of faith in their daughters' abilities, boosting their self-assurance and enabling them to embrace their individual qualities.

6. Shaping Identity And Self-Perception:

Fathers have a significant influence on their daughters' sense of identity. They help their daughters develop a healthy self-perception by helping them recognize their worth. The relationship between fathers and daughters often impacts the way in which girls perceive themselves and their place in the world. Fathers help their daughters develop a strong sense of self, in the same vein encouraging resilience and confidence.

7. Lifelong Connection And Influence:

The relationship between fathers and daughters is enduring and transcends the passage of time. The bond between fathers and daughters endures even as they mature into adults, and fathers continue to be a source of guidance, support, and affection. Even when they are not physically present, their teachings and example continue to have a lasting impact on the relationships or choices their daughters make throughout their lives.

8. Self-Esteem And Self-Confidence:

It is impossible to overstate the importance of the father-daughter relationship in promoting self-esteem and self-confidence. A daughter's self-perception is shaped by her fathers' affirming words, support, and show of faith in her abilities. Daughters who get constant encouragement and affirmation from their fathers are more likely to grow in self-esteem and self-assurance. The presence of fathers as role models and mentors encourages daughters to take chances, pursue their passions, and persevere in the face of adversity.

9. Establishing Boundaries And Building Independence:

The father-daughter connection is essential in developing sense of boundaries and independence. Daughters benefit from the structure and discipline provided by their fathers, who also teach them important life skills about responsibility, accountability, and decision-making. By encouraging daughters to follow their own interests, while providing a safety net of support and guidance, fathers help them in navigating the challenges of autonomy.

10. Relationships Across Generations:

A father and daughter relationship goes beyond just the direct bond between the two people. It carries the weight of intergenerational ties and family history. Fathers transmit values, customs, and cultural legacy to their daughters, acting as a link between the past, present, and future. This link to family origins increases daughters' sense of belonging and identity, presenting them with a rich tapestry of heritage from which to draw.

11. Impact On Relationships:

The importance of the father-daughter connection extends to the relationships that girls establish and uphold throughout their lives. The connection formed with fathers serves as a foundation for future relationships, influencing daughters' expectations, trust, and communication patterns. A positive father-daughter relationship can foster a healthy relationship dynamic, but girls may face difficulties in their relationships if their fathers were absent, distant or uninvolved in their lives.

12. Encouraging Emotional Expression:

Fathers play a vital role in encouraging their daughters to express their emotions. They educate their daughters that it is appropriate to feel a range of emotions and acknowledge their feelings. By encouraging emotional expression, father help their daughters establish a healthy connection with their emotions, developing their emotional intelligence and resilience in the process. With this encouragement daughters are better equipped to deal with difficulties and navigate their emotional landscapes.

13. Modeling Emotional Regulation:

Fathers serve as role models for emotional regulation to their daughters. By demonstrating appropriate ways to manage and express emotions, fathers provide their daughters with the essential tools for managing life's ups and downs. By maintaining composure in the face of difficulty, handling conflicts with calmness, and communicating their feelings clearly, fathers teach their girls with valuable life skills and help them develop their own emotional responses.

14. Instilling Values And Ethics:

Fathers play a key role in helping their daughters develop strong moral values. They instill in their daughters a sense of right and wrong, educate them on empathy and compassion, and help them develop a strong moral compass. Fathers help mold their daughters' character by demonstrating these ideals in their own behavior, thereby, helping their daughters grow into kind, responsible, and ethical individuals.

15. Encouraging Personal Growth And Self-Discovery:

Fathers encourage their daughters' quests for personal development and self-discovery They inspire their girls to follow their dreams, explore their hobbies, and take risks in life. Fathers give their daughters a feeling of self-belief in their abilities, encouraging them to venture outside of their comfort zones and seize new opportunities. Their encouragement and support help their daughters develop resilience and healthy sense of self.

CHAPTER THREE

How Social, Cultural, And Family Factors Affect How Daughter Grief The Loss Of A Father

The process of grieving the loss of a father can be influenced by a variety of elements beyond individual factors, such as societal, cultural, and familial dynamics. These factors have a big impact on how adult daughters respond emotionally as they walk through the grieving and healing process. Understanding how these outside factors can affect a daughter's complex emotional responses to the loss of a father can be incredibly insightful.

That said, let's take a look at some of the external factors that can influence daughters' grief over the loss of a father:

1. Cultural Influences:

Cultural influences have a significant impact on how people experience and express loss. Regarding death and grieving, many cultures have different beliefs, rituals, and customs around it. The ways in which adult daughters mourn the loss of their fathers may vary depending on certain cultural practices. Cultural expectations may influence certain mourning practices, such as grieving periods, rituals, or how one expresses grief. Emotional responses and coping methods can also be influenced by cultural views on stoicism, the afterlife, or the role of daughters in the period of grieving. Understanding one's cultural setting can help daughters navigate the interplay between personal grief and cultural expectations, striking a balance that suits their specific needs and beliefs.

2. Societal Influences:

The general society has an impact on how adult girls feel after losing a father. How daughters handle their loss can be influenced by social conventions and expectations around grief, such as the length of mourning or the expression of emotions. The healing process might be hampered by societal pressure to "move on" quickly or to suppress emotions. Additionally, social perspectives on grieving and community-based support systems can either help or hinder the mental well-being of adult daughters. Daughters can be empowered to accept their individual grieving journeys and seek care that fits their needs by recognizing and questioning societal norms and standards.

3. Familial Influences:

The emotional responses of adult daughters to the loss of a father can be greatly influenced by the family setting in which they were nurtured. Every family has its own unique dynamics, ways of communicating, and beliefs on grieving. These familial factors can have an impact on how daughters are permitted or encouraged to express their emotions, seek help, or participate in rituals of remembrance Family relationships and dynamics, both with the father and with other family members, can also have an influence on the grieving process. For instance, the complexity and intensity of emotional responses might be influenced by the presence of strained relationships, unresolved issues, or strong family support. Understanding and acknowledging familial influences can help daughters navigate their grief within the framework of their family dynamics, promoting healing and healthy ways to cope.

4. Intersecting Identities:

Intersecting identities add further complexity to the way that cultural, social, and family factors affect emotional responses to loss. The loss of a father can be impacted by factors such as race, ethnicity, religion, gender, and socioeconomic status, thereby affecting the emotional landscape in different ways. These intertwined identities have the potential to affect how grieving is perceived and experienced, as well as the accessibility of culturally appropriate support networks. It may be more difficult for grieving adult daughters from marginalized communities to get help and discover services that are appropriate to their cultures. Understanding the nuances of intersecting identities can help daughters handle the unique challenges they might have throughout their grieving process.

5. Intergenerational Grief:

In families, the loss of a father can also cause intergenerational grief. It is possible for adult daughters to feel the weight of their mothers' grief as well as the grief of their siblings, grandparents, and other family members. Daughters who recognize and understand the interconnectivity of the family's grief can better manage their own emotions while providing support to others. It creates avenues for healing and collective remembrance, fostering sense of solidarity and connection amongst family members.

6. Cultural And Interpersonal Expectations Of Strength:

Cultural and interpersonal expectations of strength could impact how a person, especially adult daughters, feels after the loss of their father. Daughters may experience pressure to take on caregiver duties, maintain stability, or serve as the backbone of their loved ones. These demands may be made out of love and obligation, but they may also add to the emotional stress daughters feel. In order to manage these expectations and allow the processing of one's grief, it is necessary for daughters to recognize the need for self-care, establishing boundaries, and seeking help.

By talking about the effects of cultural, social, and family factors on emotional responses, adult daughters can better grasp the complex nature of their grieving experiences. It permits a more nuanced exploration of their emotions, views, and coping mechanisms. By acknowledging the impact of outside factors, daughters can develop self-compassion, make intelligent decisions about their healing process, and find comfort in interacting with supportive communities that value their unique experiences.

CHAPTER FOUR

Understanding The Different Stages Of Grief For Daughters After The Loss Of A Father

Grief is a diverse and intricate process that frequently progresses through several emotional phases. These phases, which are commonly known as the Kübler-Ross model, offer a framework for understanding the range of emotions experienced by individuals who have lost a loved one, including daughters who have lost their fathers. For daughters grieving the loss of a father, the emotional stages of grief include:

1. Shock:

The initial reaction to losing a father is usually shock. This stage is characterized by a sensation of emotional and mental numbness, as well as a sense of disbelief and being confused or disoriented. Daughters who have just lost their fathers could find themselves in shock as they try to process what has happened.

During this period, daughters often go through a variety of emotional and physical reactions. They might have a feeling of disconnect from their environment or the happenings around them. It could be difficult for them to come to terms with the gravity of the loss, which might cause them to momentarily lose touch with their feelings. This emotional numbness can act as a coping mechanism, helping individuals gradually transition to the overwhelming reality of their father's loss.

Physical symptoms, including a fast heartbeat, shortness of breath, nausea, or feeling lightheaded, can also be signs of shock. These physiological reactions are the body's way of adjusting to the sudden and devastating impact of the loss.

In this period, daughters may find it challenging to articulate their feelings or effectively communicate their needs. They may look detached or unresponsive, which others might misinterpret as indifference or a lack of grief. However, it is critical for one to understand that shock is a natural and temporary response to a big loss, and it functions as a protective mechanism that helps individuals gradually process their grief in a controlled manner.

The period of shock requires daughters and those who support them to be patient, kind, and understanding. They can get over this first stage of grief when provided with a safe and supportive environment where they can express their emotions without fear of judgment.

2. Denial:

Denial is a typical emotional stage in the grieving process, especially after the loss of a father. It is a form of defense that at first protects people from the devastating truth of the loss, enabling them to deal with the grief in manageable doses. Daughters may struggle to accept the reality of their father's absence and may refuse to acknowledge the full extent of the loss during this period of denial.

In this stage, daughters could start thinking and acting in ways that seek to shield them from the awful truth. They may delude themselves into thinking their father is still alive or that the loss is just temporary, holding out hope for a turnaround, or insisting it can't be true. Denial enables daughters to cope with the emotional turmoil and digest the loss at their own pace.

It is crucial to remember that denial is a normal and appropriate response to loss, offering a momentary escape from the intensity of grief. However, long-term denial can hinder healing by stopping daughters from confronting their emotions and processing their losses. Daughters must be able to identify and acknowledge the denial stage while easing towards acceptance.

During this time, support from family, friends, or experts is essential. Family members can serve as a comforting, empathetic presence, reassuring daughters of their love while gently urging them to face the reality of the loss. Daughters who are in denial may gradually let go of it and start the healing process by creating a safe space for open and honest conversation.

Daughters could advance in the grieving process as they progressively come to terms with the reality of their father's loss. It's crucial to understand that accepting a loss does not entail forgetting about it or downplaying its significance. Instead, it represents a readiness to accept reality and set off on a path of healing and adaptation.

3. Anger:

Grieving daughters may feel a variety of intense emotions, such as frustration, resentment, and even anger. The anger may be directed in a number of directions, including towards oneself, their fathers, the circumstances surrounding the loss, or even a higher power.

Daughters could start to feel enraged and wonder why this loss happened. They might also start to experience a sense of injustice during this period. They could be angry with themselves for things they haven't said or done, at their fathers for leaving them, or at others who may have been involved in the circumstances that led to the loss. This anger is a normal reaction to the pain and turmoil brought on by their fathers' absence.

It is critical to acknowledge that anger is a valid and necessary aspect of the grieving process. It is a means for daughters to express and process their emotions, as well as cope with the sense of powerlessness that often comes with loss. Anger may serve as an outlet for the pain and resentment that are difficult to express in other ways.

During this state, finding healthy and productive ways to vent and channel their anger is important for daughters.

4. Bargaining:

During this stage, daughters may indulge in "what if" or "if only" thinking, seeking to bargain with themselves, a higher power, or even their fathers in order to change the outcome or make sense of the loss.

During the bargaining stage, daughters could revisit the past and consider whether there was anything they might have done to prevent or alter the outcome. They could feel guilty or regretful because they think their father's absence might have been averted if they had done something differently or made a different choice. This stage is often marked by a strong desire for the past to be changed or for things to go back to the way they were.

It is crucial to understand that bargaining is a common response to the overwhelming feelings of powerlessness and loss people feel. It gives daughters a sense of control and helps them make sense of the incomprehensible. By engaging in bargaining, daughters are seeking meaning, searching for answers, and wrestling with the idea that there could have been a different outcome.

During this stage, daughters must strike a difficult balance between embracing the reality of the loss and recognizing their yearning for things to be different. They may find peace in reminiscing about their relationship with their fathers and acknowledging that they did their best under the circumstances. It is important to let go of self-blame and realize that you had no influence over the outcome.

As they move through the stage of bargaining, daughters may start to understand that they cannot undo the past and that the loss is a permanent part of their lives. This insight might cause a shift in perspective from the "what if" frame of mind to accepting the lessons from the relationship with their father and finding value in his memory. Daughters might begin to find closure and peace with the past by going through this process.

5. Depression:

Depression is a typical reaction to the overwhelming sense of loss and the significant changes that come along with the loss of a loved one. During this time, daughters could feel extreme sadness, emptiness, and a general sense of despair.

Daughters who are depressed may retreat from daily tasks, lose interest in or pleasure from activities they formerly enjoyed, and feel generally exhausted or unmotivated. They could suffer from sleep issues, including insomnia or excessive sleep, go through fluctuations in appetite, and have difficulty concentrating or making decisions. Daughters often feel as though they have a constant weight on their shoulders.

It's important to understand that clinical depression is different from the depression experienced throughout the mourning process, regardless of the seeming parallels in symptoms. However, it is advised to seek professional care if the symptoms persist for a long time or severely affect daily functioning.

Daughters going through this period could feel overwhelmed by the depth of their emotions and the difficulties of adjusting to life without their fathers. They could struggle with the pain of their loss, the lack of their fathers' guidance and presence, and the challenge of redefining their identities and responsibilities in the absence of a father figure.

It is critical to allow oneself to mourn, to appreciate the depth of the relationship with one's father, and to accept that healing takes time. There is no defined timeframe for the recovery from depression; each person's path through it will be unique.

As daughters advance through the stages of depression, they may begin to experience moments of lightness and optimism. They could draw comfort from shared memories, make connections with people who have suffered similar losses, and devise new ways to cope with their depression. With time and support, daughters can rise from the depths of depression and begin the process of healing and rebuilding their lives.

6. Acceptance:

After the loss of a father, acceptance is a key step in the grieving process. It marks a turning point when daughters start to accept that their father is really gone and that things will never be the same again. It is important to remember that acceptance does not mean releasing the burden of the loss or moving on; rather, it refers to finding a way to incorporate the loss into one's life and move forward with a sense of peace and understanding.

During the phase of acceptance, daughters may notice a slow change in their emotions and perspective. They start to realize that their father is no longer physically present and that their lives have been changed forever. They start to accept the loss as a permanent part of their reality, rather than resisting or denying it.

Even after acceptance, the loss of a father still hurts, and daughters are still affected by his absence. It is an acknowledgment that the loss has happened and that adjustments to the new reality need to be made. Despite the fact that daughters occasionally experience grief, longing, or sadness, they are better equipped to deal with these emotions because, now, they have a greater sense of understanding and acceptance.

Throughout the period of acceptance, daughters may find themselves reflecting on the things they have learned from their fathers and the influence their fathers have had on their lives. They could start focusing on preserving the memories and passing on the traditions of their fathers. In order to accept a loss, a daughter must find a way to incorporate it into who she is and create a new narrative that acknowledges her father's lasting impact on her life.

As they embrace acceptance, daughters start to discover a new sense of meaning and purpose in their lives. They could come to realize their own inner resilience, fortitude, and genuine appreciation for the time they spent with their fathers. Although the loss will always be a part of their lives, acceptance enables daughters to go on with a newfound sense of optimism, resilience, and the capacity to find joy and fulfillment in the present.

By reaching the stage of acceptance, daughters can rewrite their stories in a way that acknowledges their fathers' efforts and paves the way for their continuous healing, growth, and connection to their fathers' memories.

CHAPTER FIVE

Understanding The Different Challenges Daughters Face After The Loss OF A Father

Since grief is such a personal and unique experience, adult daughters who are grieving the loss of their fathers may encounter unique struggles and experiences over the course of their journey towards healing. These challenges result from the intricate nature of the father-daughter relationship and the different roles that fathers often play in the lives of their daughters. Insights into the grief process for adult daughters can be gained by understanding and accepting these challenges.

Challenges grieving adult daughters might face include:

1. Shifting Roles And Identities:

The loss of a father can have a significant influence on an adult daughter's identity and sense of self. Fathers often serve as a source of guidance, support, and safety, and their absence may cause instability and confusion. It can be difficult and emotionally taxing for adult daughters to adjust to new roles and responsibilities, such as taking on the position of primary caretaker or decision-maker.

2. Unfinished Business And Unresolved Issues:

Adult daughters may struggle with unresolved issues or unfulfilled needs in their relationships with their fathers. This might include unfinished conversations, unexpressed feelings, and unfulfilled aspirations. In light of the loss, daughters may experience regret, shame, or despair as they long for the chance to confront these issues and find closure.

3. Changing Family Dynamics:

The loss of a father can have a big effect on how the family structure works, especially if the daughter takes on a new responsibility. Taking on caregiving responsibilities for other family members or negotiating changes in relationships with siblings or extended family members could be part of the challenges that adult daughters encounter. While grieving the loss of a father, adjusting to these new dynamics can be extremely difficult and need for additional support.

4. Reassessing Life Goals And Priorities:

This self-examination may inspire adult daughters to make substantial lifestyle changes. They might feel pressured to reevaluate their personal goals, their relationships, and their chosen career. The loss of a father can act as a motivator for introspection and a renewed sense of purpose. As grieving daughters deal with these changes, it can leave them feeling vulnerable and insecure.

5. Dealing With Society Expectations:

How people should grieve and mourn the loss of a parent is often subject to social standards and expectations. The pressure to "move on" or "be strong" could may be placed on adult daughters, which can be dismissive of their grieving process. They may feel compelled to put on a strong front or suppress their feelings in order to avoid criticism or misunderstanding from others. Regardless of what society expects, it is crucial for adult daughters to respect their own path towards healing and discover effective methods to deal with their grief.

6. Complex Emotions AndConflicting Roles:

The connection between a father and daughter is multifaceted, comprising love, affection, reverence, dependency, and, at times, complications. During the grieving process, adult daughters may feel a variety of emotions, including extreme sadness, rage, guilt, and ambivalence. They could struggle with the loss of the future experiences they had envisioned as well as mixed emotions of love and resentment towards their fathers. It takes help, understanding, and self-compassion to navigate these difficult emotions.

7. Long-Term Effects On Relationships:

The relationships that adult daughters have with other people might be adversely affected by the loss of a father. The relationships they have with siblings, extended family members, or even their own children could alter. Grief may cause both distance or intimacy as family members may grieve differently or fail to communicate properly about their shared loss. For adult daughters to manage these transitions and cultivate healthy relationships, they must look for supportive relationships as well as open and empathetic communication.

8. Impact On Career AndAchievement:

Fathers often support their daughters in pursuing their academic and professional goals. The trust they have in their daughters' ability and leadership can have an impact on their career choices and success. For a daughter, the loss of a father can trigger emotions of fear or self-doubt in pursuing her goals and dreams. The long-term impacts are examined by looking at how career paths, goals, and the capacity to face career challenges have been impacted by the loss of a father. It also stresses the value of creating a solid support system, seeking mentors, and developing confidence when pursuing both personal and professional goals.

9. Ambiguous Loss:

Adult daughters often suffer from ambiguous loss, when their father is emotionally present but physically absent, or vice versa. This form of loss can be especially difficult to deal with due to unresolved grief and a lack of closure. Adult daughters may struggle with conflicting emotions, memories, and unresolved problems, which can make grief more difficult and necessitate special coping mechanisms.

10. Gender-Related Expectations:

Gender norms and societal expectations can make the grieving process even more complicated. The pressure adult daughters may experience to be strong, stoic, or caregivers for others can make it difficult for them to express their grief and ask for help. It's critical to question these assumptions and give oneself permission to handle emotions honestly and without bias.

11. Emotional Regulation AndCoping Skill:

Fathers offer daughters emotional guidance and encouragement, which helps them develop good coping mechanisms and manage their emotions better. A daughter's capacity to properly manage and control emotions might be impacted by the absence of a father. Daughters may have trouble managing stress, anxiety, or intense emotions if they lack emotional resilience. Dealing with the long-term impact of father loss involves recognizing potential challenges with managing emotions and creating plans for self-care, emotional wellbeing, and building resilience.

12. Impact On Parenting AndFamily Dynamics:

A daughter's perspective and knowledge of parenting and family dynamics may be impacted by the absence of a father. A daughter's outlook on motherhood or her own desire for a family may be influenced by the loss of her father. In order to understand the long-term effects, it is important to consider how father loss has impacted parenting styles, attachment patterns, and the development of positive family relationships. It emphasizes how crucial it is to be conscious of oneself, seek guidance, and break generational stereotypes in order to create environment that are loving and positive for next generations.

CHAPTER SIX

How The Loss OF A Father Impacts On Daughters In Their Intimate Relationship, Friendships, And Family Relationships

The relationships that adult daughters have with their spouses, friends, and other family members can be severely impacted by the loss of a father. Understanding and acknowledging the impacts is critical for understanding the intricacies and challenges that can emerge. That said, here are the different relationship dynamics that can be impacted by the loss of a father:

1. Partners/Spouses:

The dynamics of a romantic partnership or marriage can be impacted by the loss of a father. As they negotiate their grief, adult daughters could notice changes in their emotional state, communication patterns, or levels of intimacy. The grieving process can cause swings in their emotional availability, and their partners may need to adjust to their shifting needs. Maintaining a strong positive relationship during this time requires open and honest communication, empathy, and patience.

2. Siblings:

The relationships between adult daughters and their siblings can be severely impacted by the loss of a father. Even while siblings may have gone through the same kinds of losses, their personal grieving processes might vary. There can be differences in the coping methods, emotions, and ways that each sibling expresses their grief. In sibling relationships, this may result in both emotional support or potential conflicts. To make stronger the bonds with siblings, it might be helpful to acknowledge and respect each sibling's own grieving process, encourage open communication, and look for opportunities for group therapy.

3. Mother-Daughter Relationship:

The loss of a father can have a big impact on a mother and daughter's relationship. Adult daughters could see their mothers struggling with emotional ups and downs. The dynamics between mother and daughter may change as they walk their grieving journey together. It's possible for adult daughters to play a supporting role for their mothers by offering them empathy and compassion. However, given how differently individuals handle grief, conflicts or tensions could also develop. It's critical for mother and daughter to have open conversations, validate each other's' experiences, and, if necessary, seek outside help.

4. Relationships With Extended Family:

The loss of a father can also have an effect on a daughter's relationships with their grandparents, aunts, uncles, and cousins. These family members could have had special bonds with the father and would be grieving their loss as well. With extended family members who understand the magnitude of their loss, adult daughters may find comfort in sharing memories, stories, and support. These familial bonds can be strengthened by keeping the lines of communication open and establishing chances for collective healing and remembrance.

5. Friendships:

The loss of a father can also have a big impact on friendships. Adult daughters may discover that their grief affects their ability to partake fully in social activities, maintain regular communication, or getting involved with friendship dynamic. Genuine friends will be patient, understanding, and supportive at this difficult time. For adult daughters, connecting with people who have endured a similar loss or who can offer a safe environment for honest and empathetic conversations about their grief can bring comfort to them.

6. Parenting:

The loss of a father can have a significant influence on the parenting experiences of adult daughters who are themselves parents. They could experience difficulties coping with their own grief while providing emotional support to their children who are also grieving. To make sure they are properly supporting their children's emotional well-being while also caring to their own needs, adult daughters can reach out for guidance and help through parenting resources, therapy, or support groups.

CHAPTER SEVEN

Different Roles And Responsibilities Taken On By Adult Daughters After The Loss Of A Father

The dynamics of the family can change significantly when a father passes away, and adult daughters often find themselves taking on new roles and responsibilities. Their lives may be affected in various ways by these new responsibilities, necessitating changes and adaptations. Some of the responsibilities that will befall adult daughters after the loss of a father include:

1. Caregiving For Other Family Members:

After the loss of a father, adult daughters might take on the caregiving role for other family members, such as elderly relatives, younger siblings, or grieving mother. They may end up being the main person others turn to for emotional support, useful advice, and decision-making. It can be difficult for adult daughters to balance their own grief with the needs of others, and so in order to avoid burnout, it is important that they prioritize self-care and seek support themselves.

2. Financial Management:

In some circumstances, adult daughters may need to take on responsibilities for handling finances and making decisions. This may entail managing assets, taking care of the father's estate, or helping the family with budgeting and financial planning. The increased responsibility of dealing with financial issues can be stressful, and seeking expert guidance or support can be useful in ensuring financial stability throughout this transition.

3. Legal and Administrative Tasks:

After the loss of a father, adult daughters may also find themselves handling a variety of legal and administrative tasks. This may entail organizing paperwork, contacting necessary authorities, updating legal documents, and facilitating the smooth transition of responsibilities and obligations. Adult daughters can navigate these tasks successfully by consulting professionals or seeking advice from support networks.

4. Emotional Support For Siblings:

If there are siblings involved, adult daughters may take on a massive role of providing emotional support and guidance to their brothers and sisters. This might entail helping younger siblings cope with grief, addressing their questions, and providing a sense of stability and security. Adult daughters may need to create an enabling environment where siblings feel safe expressing their emotions while dealing with the loss.

5. Mediating Family relationships:

The loss of a father can often strain family relationships or create conflicts. Adult daughters may find themselves in a position where they need to mediate and stimulate conversations amongst family members, ensuring that everyone's needs and emotions are acknowledged and respected. Playing this role requires empathy, diplomacy, and excellent communication skills in order to foster understanding and harmony within the family.

6. Parenting And Nurturing Roles:

Adult daughters who are also mothers may have a dual duty of grieving the loss of their father while catering to their own children's emotional needs. This can be extremely draining, as they seek to provide stability and support to their children while processing their own grief. Navigating this difficult position may be made easier by maintaining open lines of communication, seeking for advice from trustworthy sources, and establishing a safe environment for kids to express their feelings.

7. Continuity Of Family Traditions And Rituals:

Adult daughters may take on the task of preserving and sustaining family traditions and rituals that were important to their father. This might involve celebrating holidays, maintaining contacts with extended family members, and upholding cultural or religious rituals. By guaranteeing the continuation of these traditions, adult daughters help to commemorate their father's memory and promote a sense of stability and connection within the family.

8. Balancing Personal And Professional Life:

Adult daughters may struggle to strike a balance between their own grief and the pressures of their professions. It might be difficult to balance the emotional effects paternal loss with responsibilities at work. Adult daughters need to practice self-compassion, communicate their needs to bosses or coworkers, and seek accommodations or help if necessary. In this trying time, maintaining a healthy work-life balance will benefit their general wellbeing.

9. Household Management:

Without their father, adult daughters may be forced to take on decision-making and household management tasks. This may involve activities like making important financial decisions, overseeing home maintenance, and planning family schedules. As this can be a steep learning experience, it may be helpful for adult daughters to seek advice from reliable advisers, family members, or support networks as they adjust to these new responsibilities.

10. Personal And Family Advocacy:

After the loss of their father, adult daughters may need to speak out for their personal needs as well as the needs of their family. In order to do this, they might need to communicate with legal authorities, insurance companies, or health care providers. Adult daughters can be empowered in this role by acquiring advocacy skills, which can be crucial in ensuring that the interests of their family are protected.

11. Upholding the Father's Legacy:

Adult daughters may be tasked with upholding and preserving their father's legacy. This could involve keeping in touch with their father's acquaintances or peers, carrying on his humanitarian works or pastimes, or preserving family lore and memories. By actively sustaining his legacy, adult daughters preserve their father's presence and ensure that his impact is remembered and honored.

CHAPTER EIGHT

6 Effective Strategies On Coping With The Loss Of A Father For Daughters

For daughters, dealing with grief following the loss of a father can be a very difficult and emotionally stressful process. During this tough period, it is important to explore effective coping skills and support systems if you want to find comfort, healing, and resilience. Here are some effective coping methods adult daughters can implement when dealing with the loss of a father:

1. Seek For Emotional Support

Navigating the grieving process following the loss of a father requires seeking emotional support. Having a supportive network can provide comfort, understanding, and validation when navigating the intense emotions and complexity of grieving. Here are different ways grieving adult daughters can get emotional support:

- **Reaching out to Loved Ones:** It's important to rely on the support of reliable family members and friends when going through a difficult moment. Talk to them about your thoughts, feelings and memories. Give yourself permission to be vulnerable and be honest about your feelings. Those who love you will be there for you, ready to listen, provide a shoulder to lean on, and offer compassionate support.

- **Joining support groups:** Consider joining grief support groups for daughters who have lost their fathers. These gatherings offer a safe environment where members can connect with those going through similar losses, who understand the struggles of losing a father. These groups provide you the opportunity to share your experiences, gain insight from others, and get helpful guidance and support.

- **Seek professional help:** Grief can be an intense and difficult process, and there can be moments when professional help is required. Specialists in bereavement such as grief counselors, therapists, or psychologists can provide a compassionate and supportive environment where you can talk about your feelings, work through your loss, and come up with coping mechanisms. They can provide guidance and approaches aimed at to your specific needs, allowing you to more successfully traverse the emotional landscape.

- **Joining online groups:** In addition to in-person support, there are a ton of online forums and groups where daughters who are grieving the loss of a father can connect. These online communities offer a place where daughters connect virtually to share advice and find comfort in the words of those who have been through similar experiences. Participating in online communities can provide daughters with a sense of community and support, especially if they don't have easy access to local support groups.

- **Consider grief counseling for children:** If you have kids who are also mourning the loss of their grandfather, you might want to think about grief counseling for them. It's necessary to attend to their emotional needs as well. Children may find it difficult to express their emotions or understand the complexities of loss. Children who need age-appropriate support, resources, and a safe environment to express their feelings and process their loss can benefit greatly from grief therapy designed especially for them.

- **Express your needs:** It is important that you communicate your emotional needs to your circle of support. Tell your loved ones how they can best support you, whether it's by lending a listening ear, giving you a comforting embrace, or just being present. Sometimes, unless you communicate your needs and preferences, others might not know how best to help you. Open and honest communication can lead to stronger bonds and more meaningful support.

2. Engage In Self-Care:

Self-care is critical to navigating the grieving process after the loss of a father. It involves actively caring for your physical, mental, and emotional wellness. Self-care is often neglected during grieving periods since one's attention is diverted to coping with practical issues and processing emotions. However, making self-care a priority is essential for your overall recovery.

Here are some effective ways to practice self-care as you go through the grieving period:

- **Make rest and sleep a priority:** Grief can be physically and emotionally draining, so it's important to make rest and sleep a priority. Create a regular sleep schedule that enables you to refuel your energy. Before going to bed, establish a calm sleeping environment and practice relaxation techniques like deep breathing or gentle stretching. Getting enough sleep will improve your emotional health and provide you the energy you need to get through the grieving phase.
- **Nourish your body:** It's essential to feed your body with nourishing foods when you're grieving. Even though grief can impact one's

appetite and eating habits, it's important to maintain a balanced diet that includes a range of fresh fruits and vegetables, whole grains, and lean proteins. Avoid overindulging in harmful comfort foods or alcohol, which may provide you temporary relief, but can harm your overall health. Your physical and mental well-being can both benefit from proper eating.

- **Regular physical activity:** Studies have demonstrated that regular physical activity improves mental and emotional health. Regular exercise can help reduce stress, produce endorphins, and enhance mood. This includes walking, running, yoga, or any other sort of movement you enjoy. During the grieving process, engaging in physical exercise can also serve as a positive outlet for emotions and a way to refocus your energy.

- **Set boundaries:** During the period of grieving, it's critical to establish boundaries and preserve your emotional wellbeing. Understand that it's okay to say no to tasks or commitments that can make you feel overwhelmed or sap your energy. Put your needs first and give yourself permission to take time off. Communicate your boundaries to loved ones and let them know what you are comfortable with at this difficult time.

- **Engage in relaxation exercises:**

    Learn several techniques to help you relax your mind and body, and calm your emotions. Deep breathing techniques, mindfulness practices, meditation, and progressive muscle relaxation can all be useful methods for reducing stress and fostering emotional wellbeing. To help you regain a sense of inner balance and peace of mind, go with relaxation techniques that appeal to you and incorporate them into your daily routine.

- **Engage in activities that bring your joy:** Make time each week for the things that make you happy, comfortable, and at peace. This could involve taking part in activities you enjoy, such as listening to music, spending time in nature, reading, or watching a movie. These pursuits could provide moments of comfort and joy, as well as a momentary break from grief.

- **Practice kindness and self-compassion:** Be kind, compassionate, and understanding to yourself as you go through the grieving process. Recognize that there are many ways to experience grief and that it is a complicated and personal process. Embrace the whole spectrum of emotions without judgment or self-criticism. Practice self-compassion by speaking to yourself in a compassionate and sympathetic style, acknowledging the pain you are experiencing, and allowing yourself to grieve.

- **Engage in creative expression:** Creative expression can serve as a therapeutic tool for processing emotions and exploring your grief journey. Take part in endeavors like journaling, making art, music, or dancing. These forms of expression can help you externalize your emotions, gain insights, and find peace in the creative process.

- **Seek moments of solitude:** It can be helpful to set aside time for yourself to be alone while you're grieving. Find a quiet spot where you can be by yourself with all of your emotions and thoughts. Use this time to think, to contemplate, and to honor your father's memory. Solitude, whether through meditation, prayer, or simply being in nature, can give you a sense of inner serenity and allow for a deeper connection with yourself and your emotions.

- **Engage in self-reflection:** As you go through the grieving process, spend some time to reflect on your feelings, thoughts, and experiences. When used as a technique for self-reflection, journaling can help you explore your feelings, gain new perspective, and track your progress through time. By reflecting on your journey, you can see patterns, triggers, and places where you've changed or can benefit from additional support. Additionally, it can serve as a reminder of your resilience and the progress that you have made.

- **Participate in soul-nurturing activities:** Take part in soul-nourishing activities that make you feel at ease and peaceful. This might include spending time in nature, practicing spirituality or religious rituals, engaging with your faith community, or doing acts of kindness and service. During the grieving process, finding activities that are in line with your values and give you a sense of purpose and connection can be soothing and therapeutic.

3. Express And Process Emotions:

Navigating through grief following the loss of a father requires the ability to express and process emotions. You can aid healing and help yourself make sense of your grief by allowing yourself to acknowledge, express, and explore your feelings. Here are effective steps you can take to achieve this:

- **Establish a safe space:** Find a comfortable and safe place where you can freely express your feelings. This might be a private location in your house, a specific area for journaling, or a warm therapy setting. By creating a safe space, you can express your emotions openly and honestly without fear of ridicule or interruption.
- **Identify and label your emotions:** Give yourself some time to identify and label what you're feeling at the moment. Grief may elicit a

wide range of feelings, including grief, anger, guilt, confusion, and even relief. Allow yourself to identify and embrace these feelings as legitimate responses to your loss. You can gain clarity and obtain a deeper understanding of what you are going through by naming your emotions.

- **Journaling:** Writing in a journal can be a very effective way to process your emotions. Schedule writing time to capture your thoughts, emotions, and reflections. Use your journal as a safe place to examine every aspect of your grieving process. You can write about your memories of your father, your feelings upon his passing, and the emotions that you feel.

4. Engage In Self-Compassion Exercises:

One of the most important steps in healing after the loss of a father is to engage in self-compassion exercises. It entails being kind, considerate, and accepting of oneself through this difficult phase. To practice effective self-compassion, do the following:

- **Acknowledge your pain:** Recognize the great suffering and anguish that the loss of your father has brought. Give yourself permission to completely accept and affirm your emotions without passing judgment. Understand that it's normal to feel a variety of different emotions, and that those emotions may change over time. You are showing yourself the care you deserve by acknowledging your pain.

- **Be honest and kind to yourself:** Be understanding of your emotions, thoughts, and behaviors. Remind yourself that grieving takes time and that having good and awful days is a normal part of the process. Just like you would to a close friend going through a tough period, offer yourself words of assurance and comfort.

- **Challenge self-critical thoughts:** During the grieving process, push back against any self-critical thoughts or judgements that you might have. Self-criticism should be replaced with self-compassionate thoughts. Remind yourself that you are trying your best and that it is natural to have difficult emotions.

- **Develop mindfulness:** Work on being mindfully present and accepting of your emotions and thoughts. Instead of attempting to change or suppress your feelings or experiences, give yourself permission to observe them. Accept the notion that pain is a normal aspect of grief and that, by accepting and overcoming it, you can gain strength and resilience.

- **Develop a habit of gratitude:** Even in the middle of your grief, consciously focus on the good aspects of your life. This can help you change your perspective and create joyful and grateful moments. Express your thanks for the memories and time you had with your father, as well as the support and love you have received from others.

5. Participate In Meaningful Activities:

One effective strategy for navigating the grieving process following the loss of a father is to participate in meaningful activities. These pursuits may provide you with a sense of accomplishment and a connection to your father's memories. To partake in meaningful activities, keep the following in mind:

- **Consider your father's hobbies and interests:** Spend some time reflecting your father's interests, hobbies, and passions. Think of things you both enjoyed doing together or things that suit his values. These pursuits can foster a sense of connection and pay tribute to his memory.

- **Pursue personal growth:** Make use of this opportunity to ponder your own growth and development. Take part in activities that foster the development of new interests, talents, or skills. This can entail starting a new pastime, signing up for a class or workshop, or going after a long-held ambition. You can find a sense of fulfillment and purpose in your own life by focusing on personal development.

- **Volunteer or give back:** Think about contributing your time or resources to causes that are important to you or that your father believed in. Giving back to the community or helping those in need can give you a sense of fulfillment and provide your emotions a healthy outlet. It can also be an opportunity to remember and honor your father's generosity and compassion.

- **Engage in meaningful rituals:**
Create rituals or traditions that are special to both you and your father. This can entail setting aside particular days or times to pay tribute to his memory, such as by lighting a candle, penning a letter, or visiting to a special place. Participating in these rituals can provide you with a sense of connection and create a place for reflection and remembrance.

6. Use Rituals And Symbolism:

After the loss of a father, rituals and symbolism may be very effective tools for healing and paying tribute to his memory. They offer a concrete and profound way to express your grief, connect with your feelings, and find solace. Here are the things you can do when deploying rituals and symbolism as a means to cope with grief:

- **Establish personal rituals:** Create rituals for yourself that are important to you and your relationship with your father. You can make these rituals as basic or as complex as you choose. It can entail visiting a place that was significant to both of you, setting up a special time for thought and recollection, or lighting a candle each day in his memory. Personal rituals give life some order and provide you the space to honor your father.

- **Pick dates for commemoration:** Designate particular dates or anniversaries to commemorate your father's life. This might be his birthday, his anniversary of his passing, or any other important events that are meaningful to you. On these days, you can partake in creative activities, get together with loved ones, or take some time for introspection and remembrance. Commemorative days work as potent reminders to celebrate your father's life and the influence he had on you.

- **Incorporate symbolic objects:** Take into account including symbolic objects in your grief process. These items might hold significant personal importance to you and act as a tangible reminder of your father's role in your life. It might be a possession of his, a piece of jewelry, a picture, or anything else that captures the spirit of him. These items can help you feel at ease and connected to your father.

- **Engage in sacred spaces:** Find or create places that are peaceful and sacred to you. This could be a special space in your home, a serene area of nature, or a house of worship. You can utilize these areas as getaways where you can go to think, relax, and connect with your emotions. By purposefully establishing sacred spaces, you allow healing and contemplation into your grief experience.

- **Incorporate symbolic activities:** Include symbolic activities in your process of recovery. Writing letters to your father, launching messages or balloons into the sky, planting a tree in his honor, or performing deeds of kindness might all fall under this category. By engaging in symbolic actions, you can also express your feelings, honor your father's legacy, and take comfort in the symbolic meaning of these gestures.

- **Seek cultural or spiritual practices:** Engage in cultural or spiritual traditions that align with your principles and values. These customs could take the form of prayers, rites, or ceremonies unique to your religion or culture. By partaking in these rituals, you might feel more connected to your roots and develop a framework for dealing with loss, while finding comfort in your cultural or spiritual community.

- **Perform rituals with those you love:** Participate in the rituals and symbolic acts that have importance for you with your family and loved ones. Encourage them to share their own rituals or create new ones together. As you travel the path of healing together, sharing these experiences with your family can help everyone feel more connected, supportive, and understanding of one another.

- **Allow rituals to evolve:** Be willing to let your rituals and symbolic practices change over time. Your rituals could evolve as you deal with and process your grief. Accept the freedom to alter or develop new rituals that continue to suit your needs and pay tribute to your father in a way that seems genuine to you.

CHAPTER NINE

13 Profound Ways Daughters Can Honor And Preserve The Memories Of Their Fathers

The loss of a father provides an opportunity to embrace and honor his memories while also finding meaningful ways to continue his legacy. Here are some ideas for honoring a father's memories and keeping his spirit alive:

1. Sharing Memories and Stories:

Sharing stories and memories with loved ones is a powerful way to honor a father's memory. Gather family and friends to reminisce about memorable experiences, tales, and lessons learnt from the father. By telling these stories, you help people connect with him and remember him in a meaningful way, while also preserving his memory.

2. Creating A Memorial:

Setting up a real or virtual memorial can serve as a concrete reminder of a father's presence and the influence he had on other people's lives. A memorial plaque, a special area in the house, a social media profile, or an online memorial website can all serve as options for this. It serves as a common place for family and friends to come, share memories, and honor his legacy.

3. Preserving Traditions:

If the father loved any particular customs or rituals, carrying them on can be a way to pay tribute to his memory. These traditions, whether they involve celebrating holidays, taking part in yearly events, or performing family rituals, can act as a reminder of his ideals, passions, and the value of family ties.

4. Philanthropy And Charitable Contributions:

Giving to charity or taking part in philanthropic endeavors in memory of your father can be a touching way to honor him. Consider donating to charities or groups that reflect his values or were important to him. This allows his legacy to live on through acts of kindness and making a positive impact in the world.

5. Engaging In Shared Interests:

Participating in hobbies, interests, or pastimes that your father enjoyed could serve as a way to continue carrying on his legacy. This could involve engaging in creative pursuits, engaging in sports, or immersing oneself in activities that were important to him. By continuing to pursue these common interests, you can honor your father's memory while also finding satisfaction in them.

6. Embodying His Values And Life Lessons:

One of the most powerful ways to pay tribute to a father's memory is by embodying the principles and values he imparted. Reflect on the advice and wisdom he imparted and make an effort to incorporate those ideals into your own life. By upholding these principles, you not only pay tribute to your father's memory, but also make sure that his legacy continues to influence future generations.

7. Mentorship And Support:

Helping those in need of mentorship and support is another method to carry on a father's legacy. Share your father's wisdom, skills, and guidance with others who may gain from it. This can be accomplished by helping out younger members of the family, serving as a mentor in the community, or providing help and guidance to those in need. By helping others, one perpetuates the good impact their father made on their own life.

8. Preserving Family History:

Take charge of recording and preserving family history for future generations. Gather photos, papers, and items that are important to the father and the history of the family. Make a family tree, compile photos, or write a memoir that tells the story of the family. By preserving this history, the father's legacy becomes an ever-present element of the family's narrative.

9. Lifelong Learning AndPersonal Development:

A daughter can honor her father's memory by embracing a commitment to continued study and personal development. Whether it's seeking further education, learning new skills, or taking part in self-improvement activities, look for opportunities for personal growth. Individuals honor the father's belief in progress by working constantly to improve themselves and inspire others to do the same.

10. Advocacy And Awareness:

If your father had a cause or social issue that was important to him, consider sponsoring it or raising awareness in his honor. This could involve taking part in activities, funding relevant groups, or using platforms to promote positive change. By supporting the causes that your father believed in, you continue his passion and dedication to changing the world.

11. Creating An Award OrScholarship:

If it's possible, think about establishing an award or scholarship in your father's honor. This can be carried out in contexts such as educational institutions, organizations, or civic groups. Establishing scholarships or awards allow others to benefit from the father's legacy and support the causes he cherished. This also helps nurture future generations and contributes to their prosperity.

12.　Artistic Expressions:

This can be done through producing works of art, writing poetry or songs, composing music, or giving performances in honor of his memory. Artistic expressions give a strong outlet for emotions and a unique way to remember and celebrate the father's life.

13.　Keep His Memories Alive In Your Daily Life:

Look for ways to bring your father's memories into everyday activities. This could be you putting up a picture of him in your home, wearing jewelry or accessories that belonged to him, or incorporating his interests or hobbies into your own pursuits. By keeping his memory alive in your daily life, you ensure that he stays a part of your journey and continues to impact and inspire you.

CONCLUSION

This book has been an invaluable guide through the challenges of grief. We have looked at the significant impacts of father loss, the complex emotional landscape it creates, and the unique challenges encountered by adult daughters. This book's discussions on the father-daughter relationship, the phases of grieving, coping methods, and support mechanisms aim to bring consolation, understanding, and practical ideas for healing. May it be your companion as you seek to honor the legacy of your father while embracing your unique road toward healing.

Printed by Amazon Italia Logistica S.r.l.
Torrazza Piemonte (TO), Italy